CW00828165

HARRIET TUBMAN

Table of Contents

Introduction

For decades, children have learned in school that Harriet Tubman was a conductor for the underground railroad, helping slaves reach freedom. Not much else is usually discussed, and for most, the complete story of her life is a mystery. Most of this courageous and multi-faceted woman's life has largely been ignored.

Myths and rumors surround her earlier years as people try to guess where she came from and how she came to be a key player in the abolitionist movement. However, the information is available, primarily through oral history, letters, biographies written during her lifetime, and a few official documents. It takes some digging to get to the bottom of the story, but it is possible.

Harriet Tubman was born a slave but found her way to freedom. Yet, she was not satisfied to stop at caring for her own welfare. She went on to save others from the degradation and harsh conditions of slavery. Her contributions to the abolitionist cause did not end there, either. She worked with the union army, taking on dangerous assignments for the benefit of all the slaves and, indeed, for the betterment of the entire country.

Without Harriet Tubman and others who fought from the inside, the Civil War might have gone very differently. Her life was and is an inspiring example of what one person can do to right wrongs and change the world for the better.

One short book, or even several full-length biographies, cannot possibly tell the complete story of who Harriet Tubman was, nor the great lengths she went to in order to fight for a noble cause. Still, this short biography will give the reader a greater understanding and appreciation for this extraordinary figure.

Long ago, a powerhouse of a woman brought intelligence, courage, and persistence to the monumental task of overcoming slavery. Harriet Tubman inspired the people of her time, and her

example continues to speak to the human
need to see beyond our struggles to affect
change in the world.

Chapter 1

Being Araminta

Harriet Tubman was named Araminta "Minty" Ross when she was born. No one knows the exact date of her birth. In fact, she herself listed the year of her birth on different documents as 1820, 1822, and 1825, suggesting that even she did not know. This is just one example of how the institution of slavery disrupted family histories. Recently a document was uncovered that showed a payment for a midwife to deliver a slave child that many historians believe was Harriet. If this is true, her birth date would have been in February or March of 1822.

Araminta's mother, Harriet "Rit" Green, and her father, Ben Ross, were both slaves on Maryland plantations. Rit's mother, Modesty, had been brought to the United States from Africa. Araminta had heard that Modesty came from what is now Ghana, but no records survive to support this story. Rit was held by Mary Pattison Brodess, and was a cook for that family. Ben was a woodsman for his slave owner, Anthony Thompson. Brodess and Thompson married after Brodess's husband died. Mary's son, Edward, would soon turn 21, and when he did, he would take ownership of Rit and her family, but not Ben.

Ben and Rit had at least nine children together. Minty came along fifth. After Edward turned 21, he split up the family. Later, he sold Minty's sister, Mariah Ritty, to a Mississippi slave trader. The family would never see Ritty again. Edward sold two of her other sisters, Linah and Soph. When he tried to sell Minty's youngest brother, Moses, Rit hid him as long as she could. When Brodess found the child, Rit told him she would "split his head open" is he came for the child. Thus, Minty got her first exposure to the idea of standing up to a slave master.

When Minty was about five or six, Edward sent her away to work on another landowner's plantation. This was common practice, especially for a landowner like Edward, who had more slaves than he needed. Her first job was with the James Cook family, learning to weave. Cook also sent her out to check his muskrat traps, a cold, wet job that he forced her to do even when she was ill. Cook often beat her. She never learned to weave. When she came down with the measles, she was no longer useful to Cook at all, so he sent her back to Edward Brodess.

Later on, Minty went to work for a slave owner she knew as Miss Susan. Although little Minty did her best, she had never been taught how to take care of a house. Miss Susan whipped her, often several times a day. At night, Minty had to rock Miss Susan's baby's cradle. If she fell asleep and the baby cried, Miss Susan would grab the whip she kept under her pillow and beat her again.

Minty ran away from Miss Susan after her mistress saw her taste her first lump of sugar. She ran for miles, but there was nowhere for her to go, no one to take her in. She ended up hiding in a barn, fighting for the scraps that were put out for the pigs. Hungry, weak and alone, Minty went back to Miss Susan's, where she was beaten fiercely with a knotted rope. Thin, weak and injured, Minty once more needed her mother to nurse her back to health before she would be of use. Each time she recovered, she was sent off to work away from her mother. However, the worst was still to come.

Chapter 2

Injury and Premonitions

Throughout her childhood, Minty had been owned by first Mary and then Edward Brodess, even though she had spent much of the time working at other plantations. One landowner after another took her and then sent her back when she was too weak, sick, or injured to do the housework. Finally, Brodess tried to sell her. When he couldn't, he made her a field slave.

Edward hired her out to work for a landowner who was the most notorious for mistreating slaves. He beat her regularly and did not give her enough food to eat. One day, he sent a teenaged Minty along with his cook to pick up some items for him at the store.

While Minty stood waiting for the shopowner, a runaway slave came rushing into the store. Next came the overseer, who had tracked the young male slave to that location. The overseer grabbed the runaway and demanded that Minty help him hold onto the youth so he could beat him. Minty refused.

The overseer picked up a heavy weight and lobbed it at the young black man. The weight missed the runaway, though, and bashed into Minty's head. She fell to the ground but eventually revived enough to be taken back to the plantation. There, other slaves found a place for her to sit at a loom, the only seat available. No doctor was sent to see to her injuries. After two days in and out of consciousness, she was sent back to work in the fields. As she worked, blood continued to flow from her head wound.

Medical historians suggest that her injury resulted in temporal lobe epilepsy due to the signs she displayed afterward. She had vivid dreams, which she remembered and relied on to guide her in her life. She had waking visions that varied from the horrifying to the beautiful. Often when she was busy doing something, she would fall fast asleep. Some have suggested this was narcolepsy, but the consensus is that it was a symptom of the temporal lobe epilepsy. She also had severe headaches and even seizures. All these symptoms continued for the rest of her life.

Harriet Tubman was a deeply religious woman, but her faith was her own unique mixture of African, Baptist, Catholic, and Methodist faiths she had encountered. Her premonitions and visions sometimes centered on religious themes. Although Minty was exposed to the New Testament, she could not accept the passages that instructed slaves to be obedient to their masters. She became fascinated with the Old Testament stories of deliverance, instead.

Beyond the Bible passages that she memorized at church, Minty, like most slaves, had no formal education and little instruction in anything outside of the ins and outs of being a slave. A part of the reason slave owners did not want slaves to read or write was that if they could, they would be able to forge their masters' signatures on passes so they could outwit the slave patrols that watched for fugitives. Another reason was that they believed an educated person would not go along with being a slave. However, they underestimated Harriet's natural intelligence and desire to be free. Over the years, Harriet would fool slave patrols, slave owners and slave traders many times over, regardless of her lack of formal education.

After she recovered from the injury as best she could, Edward sent her to work for John T. Stewart. Minty's father, Ben, was also working for Stewart, as were some of her brothers. She was treated better than she had been before, and she became so strong that Stewart would have her lift heavy weights as he showed her off to his friends and fellow plantation owners. Minty worked at Stewart's farm for about five or six years.
When Ben Ross's owner, Anthony Thompson, died in 1836, he left a will that allowed Ben to be freed when he was 45 years old. When he reached that approximate age, he was given 10 acres

of land nearby. He stayed in the area to be near family and worked for wages to support himself. Minty's father was now free. Soon, another free man would enter her life.

Chapter 3

Mysterious John

Historians do not know precisely when Minty Ross took the name of Harriet Tubman. While the last name probably came after her slave owner allowed her to marry John, the mystery remains as to when she chose to call herself Harriet in honor of her mother. And, John Tubman remains something of a mystery as well.

John was a free African American that Harriet knew. In Maryland, where the two both lived, there were many free blacks. It was quite common for the free people and the slaves to know each other in that part of the country. What was rare was for them to marry.

No one living knows much about how they met or how much time they spent together as a married couple. Some historians believe that the relationship between John and Harriet Tubman was a forced marriage. They were married in 1844, but the marriage could not have lasted more than a few years, because, by October 1849, Harriet had left the area. Harriet walked away from slavery that month, after a failed attempt at freedom a month earlier.

Edward allowed Harriet to work for other plantation owners because he trusted her to give him a large portion of what she earned. This was a common practice in Maryland. Harriet was so strong and able that she could do more work than most slaves could. So, she garnered a higher wage. She saved up her money and bought two oxen, which she used to make even more money.

However, Edward was broke. He needed more money than his share of her earnings. Harriet became aware that Edward meant to sell her and other slaves, including two of her brothers. She began praying for Edward's death. Soon, he did die. She blamed herself and her angry prayer.

Edward's daughter Eliza inherited his slaves. She wanted to sell off slaves to settle Edward's debts. Harriet and her brothers were terrified of being split up and nervous about how the new master might treat them. They decided to run away.

John, although he would have been entirely free to go with her, refused. Harriet never told anyone why he remained behind, but some historians believe he was involved with another woman, whom he did not want to leave.

Harriet was still intent on running away, however. She and her brothers walked out into the forest and past many farmhouses. Harriet had had visions of flying over trees and mountains, and her escape to freedom must have felt to her as if God himself ordained it. However, her brothers were afraid. A bounty of $50 each had been placed on their return - $100 if they were found outside Maryland. The brothers refused to go on and eventually went back, taking Harriet along with them.

In less than a month, Harriet would fly away again, this time with the help of other runaway slaves, free black people, Quakers, and abolitionists. Her flight from freedom would be a train ride on the railroad that later made her famous.

Chapter 4

First Ride on The Underground Railroad

For a woman who said she had a right to liberty or death, the Underground Railroad was the perfect vehicle. She had a good chance at freedom, but she also risked death or recapture every day she was on the trip. Historians estimate that the trip would have taken her up to five weeks, mainly on foot, for the 90-mile journey to Pennsylvania.

The Underground Railroad was, of course, not a railroad at all in the literal sense. It was a network of people to help runaway slaves along specific routes to freedom. The network did use railroad terminology to help obscure the workings of the Underground Railroad from slave owners, slave traders and slave patrols. Guides were called conductors, stops along the route were called stations or depots, and fugitives were called passengers or cargo.

Harriet did not take her brothers along this time but set off alone to face the unknown. Before she left, she sent a message to her mother in the form of a song that included the words "I'm bound for the promised land."

Historians believe her first stop would have been in Poplar Neck, where a large contingent of Quakers made their homes. Then, as a novice to the Underground Railroad, she would probably have taken the most common route, which would have taken her along the Choptank River to Delaware and then to Pennsylvania.

Using the Underground Railroad meant she would have some places to stop and rest, but more often, she would be on her own, making her way by watching the position of the North Star in the sky. During the day, she hid in the forests she already knew so well from her time hauling logs as a slave.

Secrecy and deception were nearly always necessary for those traveling the Underground Railroad. At times, she could be in plain sight during her rest stops, but only if she posed as a slave for the family that sheltered her. These families had no intention of keeping her or even making her work hard. It was merely a ruse to fool slave hunters who might be nearby. Even when she made it to freedom, Harriet told no one about the route she took until much later, when runaway slaves were no longer using it.

When she arrived in Pennsylvania, Harriet was so relieved and excited to be free that she found herself wondering if she was even the same person. She looked at her hands and saw that she was. Yet, the world seemed fresh and beautiful as it never had before.

Harriet did not stay safely in Pennsylvania for long. For a while, she worked to save money, doing whatever various small jobs she could find. After a while, she went to New Jersey, where she could earn more money as a housekeeper and cook at a seaside hotel. Still, she missed her friends and family. Her heart ached to know that they were still slaves and not enjoying freedom as she was. Soon, she would begin making other trips to help them reach the paradise she had found for herself in the northern state.

However, before she left, the U.S. Congress passed a law that would make the Underground Railroad even more necessary. After the Fugitive Slave Law of 1850 went into effect, routes to freedom became even more treacherous. The law promised harsh punishments for anyone helping runaway slaves. Harriet knew that she was risking her life to help those she cared about so much. Undaunted, she prepared for her first journey.

Chapter 5

Harriet as Conductor

When Harriet heard that her niece Kessiah, and Kessiah's two children, were to be sold, she knew it was time to go back to the Underground Railroad to help her loved ones. This time, though, she went as a guide, or a conductor, as they were called.

Harriet made her way to where the slave auction was to be held and stayed hidden at her John Tubman's brother's house until the day of the sale. John Bowley, Kessiah's free husband, bid on her and won the bid. He took Kessiah and the children away while the auctioneer was looking away. They rode 60 miles in a log canoe to Baltimore, where they met up with Harriet, who conducted them to Philadelphia.

When Harriet arrived back home on her mission to bring her husband to her new home in Philadephia, John Tubman was already remarried to another woman. She left him behind for a second time and never attempted to reunite with him again.

Harriet was an independent, self-reliant woman. She may have felt rejected or fearful – no records exist to explain all her feelings – but she was certainly angry. She considered going to John Tubman's home to make trouble, but decided it was a bad idea, and pointless at that. And, she was determined to follow through with her quest to free as many of her family members and friends as she possibly could. So, Harriet took another group of about five slaves back with her.

Because giving direct instructions in front of others could jeopardize the Underground Railroad network, conductors used coded messages, hand signals, and even songs to let their passengers know what to do.

Harriet later told a story about how she would sing "Go Down, Moses" to let them know whether it was safe to go. She would sing the song clearly, and by all accounts, beautifully. Depending on how fast she sang it, the former slaves would know whether to move ahead or wait. Other times, she used the same song to encourage other slaves to join her. Because of this song, and because she led her people to freedom, she became known as "Moses."

Harriet had several techniques for ensuring that her passengers were safe on the Railroad. When a baby was crying enough to call attention to the fleeing slaves, Harriet would give it laudanum to quiet it. Once, she hid her passengers in the wagon of some bricklayers after telling them to talk to people on the street and sing as they hauled the wagon through town to distract those out looking for fugitive slaves.

Harriet also protected herself. When she was in public, on a train, for example, she would grab a newspaper and pretend to read. Since everyone knew Harriet Tubman could not read, they assumed it was not her. She wore disguises on her journeys, especially after she had become well-known.

On one trip, she and a group of 11 fugitive slaves found their way to the home of abolitionist Frederick Douglass. Douglass was a learned black abolitionist who wrote several books and secured the freedom of many slaves. He later commented that it was difficult feeding and hiding so many people at once, but he was happy to do it. Still, later, he wrote Harriet, commending her for her noble and courageous work on the Underground Railroad.

Harriet had faith in God to keep her safe and guide her on her journey, but she still took extra precautions to protect herself and the others she guided. She always brought along a revolver, which she used when necessary. On one trip, as the story goes, she held the gun on two slaves who were afraid to keep moving. Would she have killed them? That is hard to say, but they believed she would and started walking again.

During her time conducting on the Underground Railroad, Harriet worked with many of the most notable abolitionists. One was a free black minister. After abolitionist agents pointed the way past Dover, others ferried her and her passengers across the Chesapeake. Once there, a Quaker named Thomas Garret would get them transportation to go to a black abolitionist named William Still. Still made sure they made it beyond the United States, where the Fugitive Slave Law had made life more dangerous for fugitive slaves, and on into Canada.

Chapter 6

Canada and the Dover Eight

Canada offered something that Philadelphia, or anywhere in the U.S. for that matter, could not supply. That is, it gave former slaves assurance that they would not have to go back into slavery. The Fugitive Law of 1850 had prompted U.S. slave patrols to observe black people for signs they might be runaway slaves. They demanded black people show proof that they were either free or on an errand for their master. They wandered the cities carrying guns and leading vicious dogs, terrifying the African Americans who lived there permanently or who were on a journey to freedom.

Canada was a safe place for slaves to be, but it was also a much harsher climate than they were used to in Maryland. They had to work hard to survive, and they were not welcomed as guests in white restaurants or hotels. Still, their children could go to black schools openly and learn to read and write without fear of punishment. The African Americans had their own churches. If they were able to buy land, which was relatively cheap, they could even vote.

Whenever Harriet made her way to Canada with a cargo of former slaves, she stayed for a while to earn money to survive and to save up to bring more passengers to Canada. Harriet worked the Underground Railroad for a total of eight years, conducting a total of 10 to 13 rescue missions and leading about 70 slaves to freedom, according to some historians. Others place the number of trips at 19, and the number of slaves freed at nearer 300. In all that time, Harriet was never captured. She never lost a passenger, according to a speech she gave later in her life, and according to black abolitionist writers of her time.

During her last year as a conductor, she got word that her now free father had bought his mother. They were in trouble and the incident that caused it had become public knowledge.

Eight slaves from Maryland had escaped to Dover, Delaware. There, they were captured and put in prison. The "Dover Eight" broke out and went their separate ways before reuniting at Ben and Rit's cabin. Harriet's parents were helping the slaves escape when they were found out. When Harriet heard the news, she immediately left to help them. To save her parents from legal punishment, she guided them along the Underground Railroad to safety. They were around 70 years old when they escaped from slave territory for good. Harriet watched over them and made sure they were cared for as long as they lived.

By this time, Harriet had made a name for herself. All the well-known abolitionists had either met her or wanted to meet her. In about 1857, the year Harriet took her parents to freedom in St. Catharine's, Canada, she would meet one of the most famous abolitionists of the time.

Chapter 7

Harper's Ferry Raid

Harriet said she had a vision in which she met John Brown, the famous abolitionist who advocated violence as a means to end slavery. Whether Harriet's vision was a divine message or a human hope, it did come true in April 1858.

Harriet's friend, Reverend Jermain Loguen of New York, arranged for them to meet. Brown was so fascinated and impressed with Harriet's stories about freeing slaves that he called her "General Tubman."

John Brown believed that slaves would revolt against their masters and create a free state. His methods were nothing short of brutal, and many abolitionists such as Frederick Douglass and William Lloyd Garrison opposed his means, even if they did agree with the end goal of ending slavery.

Yet, Brown had already conducted a successful raid in Kansas when he went to see Harriet in Canada. He had plans for a new raid, this time on Harper's Ferry, Virginia. He sought Tubman's help in recruiting slaves that lived around her base of operations in Canada. Brown intended to send these former slaves into battle in Virginia.

He also made use of Tubman's vast network of allies along the Underground Railroad and among abolitionists. Her knowledge of the people and places involved was invaluable to Brown as he planned his attack. On May 8, he held a meeting to present the details of the plan.

However, the government found out about the planned attack, and Brown put it off until the fall of 1859. When it was time to make final preparations, Brown and his supporters could not find Tubman. On October 16, they went ahead with the raid on Harper's Ferry, despite Tubman's absence. The raid ended badly for Brown and his troops. Brown was charged with treason and hanged two months later.

Several reasons have been suggested as to why Harriet was not at the raid on Harper's Ferry. Some say she may have been ill due to her previous head injury. Others say she still may have been recruiting Ontario slaves for the attack. One historian suggests she was in Maryland, helping family members escape.

Finally, there is the possibility that Harriet changed her mind about supporting Brown. After all, she did not advocate violence. Perhaps Frederick Douglass, who was one of her friends and admirers, may have convinced her that Brown's way was not the best way to end slavery.

Whether Tubman changed her mind about Brown's methods or not, she praised him after his death for his commitment and sacrifice to the cause of ending slavery.

Chapter 8

A Home of Her Own

By 1858, Harriet was well-acquainted with most of the prominent abolitionist leaders. She knew abolitionists like John Brown, Frederick Douglass, Lucretia Mott, Jermaine Loguen, William Still, Thomas Garrett, Wendell Phillips, Thomas Wentworth Higginson, and William Wells Brown. She also knew freethinkers and writers like Ralph Waldo Emerson, Franklin B. Sandborn, and Bronson Alcott.

Harriet began speaking to audiences about her work on the Underground Railroad and her quest to free slaves. At first, she spoke before small audiences in people's homes. Eventually, she began speaking in public buildings for larger and larger audiences.

By all accounts, Harriet was a fascinating speaker. She told vivid and dramatic tales of her years as a slave and her experiences as an Underground Railroad conductor. She used different voices to speak for different characters in her stories and filled her speeches with emotion. She also told about things that many abolitionists could only imagine.

In 1859, another abolitionist offered to help Tubman. Senator William H. Seward offered to sell her a plot of land at the edge of Auburn, NY. The land had a small house and barn on it. Seward had sold other tracts of land to people in need, but to sell land to a fugitive slave woman was a bold move. What is more, he only asked for $25 as a first payment and set no dates for payments on the remaining balance.

Harriet agreed to his price of $1,200 for it. She promptly moved her parents out of the cold Canadian climate and into her new home in Auburn. Through the years, Harriet welcomed African Americans to her home to stop by for a while or to stay for more extended periods. Her home was a sanctuary for friends and family members who enjoyed the break from proslavery action.

Harriet now had a home, and it was filled with love and friendship. There was one thing she didn't have, though. She did not have any children of her own in her home. So, in 1862, she decided to remedy that by adopting a child. Her new daughter was 10-year-old, light-skinned Margaret Stewart. The girl looked very similar to Harriet.

How and why Harriet took Margaret is a matter of much debate and speculation. The girl's mother was free, and their home life was comfortable. Harriet may have kidnapped her, wishing for a child she never had. Alternatively, the girl may have been her own daughter, a child she might have had before she left slavery and Maryland behind.

Whatever the case, Harriet did not stay in Auburn to raise Margaret, although she visited her often, and the two were very close. The Sewards took in the child and gave her beautiful toys to play with in a spacious nursery. Frances Seward's sister Lazette, as well as others in the abolitionist movement, took care of the child as well.

Meanwhile, Harriet's popularity among abolitionists and her reputation for bravery put her in a position to have an even more significant impact on the fight for ending slavery. She was about to become a key player in the Civil War. But first, she had one more ride to conduct on the Underground Railroad.

Chapter 9

Rescuing Sis

The year was 1860. Harriet Tubman was about to make her last trip conducting the Underground Railroad. She went with a singular mission – to rescue her sister Rachel and Rachel's two children. Slave owners, slave traders, and slave patrols had now heard about her fight against slavery, so she would have to be extremely careful. She would travel in disguise, as she had for many years.

Harriet made the trip successfully, arriving safely in Dorchester County, Maryland, where she had spent her childhood. However, when she arrived, she received news she hadn't expected. Her sister Rachel had died before she got there. There were the two children, though, and Harriet meant to take them back with her.

There was one major problem, however. The only way to get the children was to pay a bribe for their release. A $30 bribe would have allowed Harriet to complete her last Underground Railroad mission successfully, in the way she envisioned it. She did not have the money and was not able to raise it in time to satisfy the person asking for the bribe. She lost the chance to save the children.

Nevertheless, true to Harriet Tubman's calling, she would not let the effort fail to bring about some good. She gathered a group of slaves and took them to freedom. She may have been heartbroken to discover that she would lose all contact with her sister's family, but she just as surely felt confident that her trip had not been wasted.

Harriet's time on the Underground Railroad had been fruitful. She could have gone on leading individual slaves to their freedom for years, except that the times were about to change. The Civil War was brewing, and Harriet changed her focus to ending slavery for all American slaves for good. She began spending more time with abolitionists. Then, she began to get acquainted with the people who would become her new mentors and contacts during the war. She had been ready to fight for freedom all along. Now, she had a chance to do it alongside a powerful antislavery advocate and a large fighting force – President Lincoln and the Union Army.

Chapter 10

Recruiter, Scout, and Spy

In 1862, a year after the Civil War began and not long after she adopted young Margaret, Harriet Tubman became active in the Civil War effort. She felt very strongly that if the Union Army won, it would signal the beginning of the end of slavery.

Tubman started by joining a group of abolitionists who were going to South Carolina to help fugitives from the South. Brigadier General David Hunter wanted Harriet to help the Union cause. John Andrew, then the Governor of Massachusetts, gave Harriet letters of introduction, allowing her to enter the Union camps and provide whatever assistance the leaders asked of her.

The Union Army had a significant presence in South Carolina, and fugitive slaves were arriving daily for safety and assistance. Harriet knew that her experiences fighting slavery would be of great assistance to the leaders, and she probably suspected that they would put her to better use later on.

For the time, though, she worked diligently to help the fugitives survive, nursing them to health and cooking nourishing food for them. She even devised an herbal remedy for dysentery that was so effective the leaders asked her to give it to all the soldiers who had the disease.

During this time, and shortly afterward, Colonel James Montgomery was working to form and train the 2nd South Carolina Volunteers unit of the Union Army. These soldiers were African Americans, many of them fugitive slaves. Tubman aided him by recruiting more black men to serve in the unit.

Although skilled nurses and cooks were crucial to the Union cause, Harriet did more than traditional woman's work. She also served as a scout and spy for Union forces. Harriet's knowledge of the southern terrain was useful to the soldiers as they planned their movements. It also helped her as she made her way behind enemy lines to find out what Confederate units were planning and doing. She observed their movements and watched for signs of trouble, always reporting back to the Union leaders.

Another facet of her experience that proved useful was her numerous contacts with black people across the South and up into Canada. She developed a vast spy network of African American contacts that the Union Army could rely on to give them information about Confederate movements and actions. Harriet, in her position as a scout for the 2nd South Carolina Volunteers, would go out into Confederate territory, posing as a slave to get to the heart of the Confederate operation. Often, it was Harriet herself who gathered the information and relayed it back to the Union officers.

Tubman was faithful to the cause of ending slavery, so, understandably, she did not wholly back President Lincoln. At first, Lincoln only wanted to stop the expansion of slavery. He initially had no intention of freeing the slaves who were already in bondage. When Montgomery formed the African American unit of volunteer soldiers, Lincoln scolded him. Harriet was angry and said that the Union Army would never win as long as Lincoln was not doing what was right and just.

In 1863, Lincoln would redeem himself in Harriet's eyes by signing the Emancipation Proclamation. In the meantime, though, Harriet would visit with Mrs. Lincoln but not with her husband. Later on, Harriet would express regret that she never met Abraham Lincoln nor even understood that he was a friend of the African American people. After the proclamation was signed, she had more work to do for the Union Army.

Chapter 11

Combahee River Raid

Colonel Montgomery made good use of the intelligence Harriet gathered for him. Her information was an essential contribution to the capture by the Union Army of Jacksonville, Florida. Later that year, she supplied more information that led Union officials to ask her to head up a raid on the Combahee River. She agreed gladly, but with one stipulation – Colonel Montgomery must be in charge and go with her on the raid.

Three gunboats started down the Combahee River carrying Montgomery, Tubman, and 300 soldiers. The boats stopped several times, to let soldiers out to comb the fields for possible recruits among the free black men, or to remove mines from the waters.

The goal of the raid was to disrupt supply lines for Confederate soldiers. They destroyed bridges and railroad tracks. They destroyed Confederate weapons. They also burned down plantations along with cotton and rice that were stored on them. Some people criticized them when it was all over, saying that they destroyed property needlessly. However, the destruction did help their cause and made it just a little bit easier for the North to win the war. Besides that, other Union soldiers were using the same tactics without the same criticisms.

As the boats made their way on the river, slaves came out of their cabins and stood watching the raid. However, they did not watch for long. They quickly realized their opportunity to escape. They came rushing toward the boats, but when they got to the shore, the ones that would not fit on the small boats sent to carry them to the gunboats were terrified they would be left behind. They clung to the small boats despite the oarsmen hitting them over their heads to push them back.

Colonel Montgomery told Harriet to sing
to the anxious crowd. Perhaps it was her
beautiful, strong voice that reassured
them. Or, maybe they knew it was Harriet,
the Underground Railroad conductor and
Union spy they trusted. Whatever the
reason, the operation moved smoothly
after that. Harriet and the troops helped
the fleeing men, women, and children
aboard.

Over 750 slaves were taken to freedom
following the raid. About 100 of them
joined the Union Army, many of them as a
result of Harriet's recruiting. In all the Civil
War era, before it and long after it, Harriet
Tubman was the only woman to have led
soldiers into an armed assault.

Harriet worked with the Union Army for
another two years. One of her most well-
known triumphs besides the Combahee
River Raid was her involvement in the
assault on the Confederate post of Fort
Wagner. During that assault, she worked
closely with Colonel Robert Gould Shaw,
who died during the battle. Harriet later
described the fighting metaphorically,
comparing it to a violent thunderstorm that

ended in a rain of blood. The Union lost the battle, but it highlighted the bravery of Tubman and the African American soldiers. One of them, William H. Carney, was awarded the first Medal of Honor ever received by a black man.

Between and after the battles, Harriet continued to take care of sick and injured soldiers. She also kept tapping into her network of spies to help Union officers strategize their next moves. She continued her service until the war was over. Then, at the end of it all, she tried to get veteran's benefits. Despite help from many high-profile abolitionists and government leaders such as Seward, she was never paid for her service - until she finally received $12 per month for it in 1899. She would only receive $8 per month as a widow's benefit after her second husband died in 1888.

Chapter 12

Second Marriage

After the Civil War, Harriet Tubman returned to her home in Auburn, New York. She ran a boarding house of sorts, taking care of sick and wounded soldiers as well as homeless former slaves and elderly black people who had no one else to call on for assistance.

One of the people who came to Tubman's boarding house was Nelson Davis. It has long been known that Davis was a wounded veteran of the Civil War. Recently, historians began digging deeper into Davis's history. Nelson had been a slave in Elizabeth City. He probably escaped slavery in about 1861, using the Underground Railroad.

There is no indication that Harriet knew him when he arrived at her boarding house. This rings true because, by the time he escaped, Harriet had stopped conducting passengers to safety and had moved on to speaking at rallies and then to her role in the Civil War.

Historians now believe that Davis was known as Nelson Charles during the time he was a slave for the George Charles family. This is partly based on a record found in the 1850 census that shows this family having a small number of slaves, one of which was a male the age that Davis would have been at that time.

Later, after he gained his freedom, Davis fought in several battles for the Union Army, including the Battle of Olustee in Florida. When the war was over, he was discharged and received veterans benefits.

After Tubman and Davis met, they quickly developed a close relationship. On March 18, 1869, Harriet and Nelson were married at a predominantly white church with many of Tubman's abolitionist friends there with them to share their moment.

After the couple became husband and wife, Harriet settled down with him. It was the time in her life when she was able to stay in one place for an extended period. Harriet and Nelson ran a brick-making business and worked Harriet's seven-acre farm.

Like Harriet, Nelson was a deeply religious person. In fact, he helped found the African Methodist Episcopal Zion Church. Harriet and Nelson spent a great deal of time at the church, socializing and being spiritually nurtured along with others in the community.

According to some accounts, Nelson and Harriet adopted a child, whom they called Gertie. Many historians overlook this story, and some deny it is true. Since the name could be a shortening of Margaret, some believe the child in their home was only the daughter Harriet adopted, whether she did so before or after she met Nelson.

Nelson contracted tuberculosis, so Harriet took care of him, calling on her experience as a Civil War nurse for guidance. During this time, another tragedy struck. On February 10, 1880, her farmhouse caught fire and was destroyed, along with all of Nelson's and Harriet's possessions. They would recover from this blow, gathering funds and rebuilding the farmhouse. But, Harriet, for all her nursing expertise, could not conquer Nelson's tuberculosis. He died in October 1888, at the age of 44.

Many of Harriet's guests at the boarding house had moved on. Her adopted daughter Margaret was grown up and had moved to a nearby home. Only her second adopted daughter, Gertie, as well as four unrelated boarders and Harriet's mother, Rit, still lived at Harriet's home.

With more time on her hands, Harriet set out on a new venture. She wanted to take care of more older adults who needed help. Her first task in this job was raising funds, a job that proved to be more difficult than she expected.

Chapter 13

Buying Gold and Other Financial Pursuits

When Harriet Tubman only needed to survive on her own, odd jobs were often enough to do that as well as help her pay for passengers on the Railroad. When she brought her parents to Auburn, raising vegetables, picking fruit, selling the produce on her property, and managing the brick-making business did the trick. She eventually had two concerns that required more money than she could make with her own two hands.

First, years before Nelson Davis died, she needed to pay for her house. Seward, who had sold her the house and land, died while Harriet still owed money for the property. She was able to raise funds and pay Seward's son the $1200 she owed.

Her other sizeable financial need was related to another one of her causes. She could not start a decent home for the aged without enough money to build or support it. She tried several techniques for raising the money, but not all of them were successful.

Her worst experience in raising funds happened when she tried to make money from the purchase of gold. Her brother, John Stewart, had met two men who claimed to have a chest full of gold that was worth $5,000. They said they would sell it at a loss to get the cash they needed. The selling price they quoted John was $2,500. Harriet believed she saw a great opportunity to buy the gold and turn a quick profit.

However, the sale was not to be. Harriet had a hard time raising the $2,500, but after promising a businessman named Anthony Shimer that she would repay it quickly, she was able to come up with the cash.

She went to meet with the men, but they told her to give them the money. They promised she would get the gold soon enough. But, Harriet was suspicious, so she would not part with the money. Then, they told her it was hidden in the woods. She went to meet the men out in the woods but demanded they open the chest and show her the gold before she gave them the cash.

The men continued to play their cruel game, telling her that they had to leave to get the key. She examined the chest and found no keyhole. Suddenly, she blacked out. When she awoke, her hands were bound. She did not know her way out of the woods and wandered for quite some time. Moreover, Shimer's money was gone. Shimer and John Stewart found her in the woods the next day. Harriet never repaid the money.

Tubman found a better way to raise money, however. She worked with biographer Sarah Bradford to update the story of her life. About four years after the Civil War ended, Bradford had written the first installment of Harriet's story in her book *Scenes from the Life of Harriet Tubman*. That book went to support

Harriet. Now, the new book, *Harriet Tubman: Moses of Her People*, went to raise funds for Tubman's home for the aged. She also gained financial support for the home when she spoke about the needs of the elderly in 1896, at the first National Association of Colored Women convention.

Harriet paid $1,450 for 25 acres of land with several buildings on it. She used one of the buildings to house the elderly. Later, she set up another of the buildings for hospital care of the aged. She called this second building John Brown Hall.

In 1903, Tubman could no longer keep the home afloat. The financial burden was just too great. So, she sold the home to the African Methodist Episcopal Zion Church, which assumed the financial responsibility for it. Harriet still worked there, caring for the residents of the buildings that became the Harriet Tubman Home for Indigent and Aged Colored People and patients of the John Brown Hall hospital in 1908. Handling money was not her forte, but caring for others was one of her greatest talents. Another was her determination to fight for the rights of the oppressed. On that score, she had yet another job to do.

Chapter 14

Women's Suffrage

Harriet Tubman's causes were primarily about helping African Americans, but beyond that, she advocated equal rights for all people. So, after her work on the Underground Railroad, in the Civil War, and, along with her work at the Harriet Tubman Home for Indigent and Aged Colored People, Harriet helped with the struggle for gender equality.

Women at that time had very few rights. Women's groups began discussing how to obtain these rights at meetings in the mid-1800s. Later, the women's suffrage movement shifted the focus to the singular task of acquiring the right to vote. Harriet was not a leader of the women's suffrage movement, but she knew its leaders well and assisted them whenever she had the opportunity.

Many of the same women who worked towards ending slavery were also members of the women's suffrage movement. Harriet met Lucretia Mott, Susan B. Anthony, Elizabeth Cady Stanton, and other women's rights advocates when they were involved in the fight to end slavery. After the Civil War was over, women's suffrage took the top spot on these women's agendas.

Harriet Tubman's main contributions to women's suffrage were the tours she went on to support the cause. She spoke at rallies, conventions, and meetings, telling the story of how she redefined the role of women through her work as a conductor on the Railroad and the positions she held with the Union Army. She won over the audiences as a masterful storyteller with firsthand experience in living under slavery and fighting for her freedom and the freedom of others.

Harriet believed that all Americans should have the right to vote, but she was particularly interested in the rights of African American women. In 1896, Harriet had lived a long life and had become quite frail. Nevertheless, she traveled to Washington, D.C. in order to speak at the first meeting of the National Association of Colored Women. There, she encouraged African American women to not only fight for the vote but to exercise that valuable right once they had it.

A time came when Susan B. Anthony supported women's right to vote over African American's right to vote. In Kansas, both issues were on the same ballot, and Anthony feared that the push to give black Americans the right to vote would take the spotlight away from women's suffrage. This thinking would not have been acceptable to Harriet, who thought that both women and men, both black and white, indeed all adult Americans should be allowed to cast votes in elections throughout the country.

Women's suffrage was not achieved until the Nineteenth Amendment to the Constitution was passed in 1920, seven years after Harriet Tubman's death. Her earlier contributions to the cause helped get women's rights into the mainstream of American thinking and gather support from African American women.

Chapter 15

Brain Surgery, Illness, and Death

Harriet Tubman had lived a remarkable life and accomplished feats others could not even imagine. Moreover, she did it all despite frequent illness and the severe physical effects of the brain trauma she suffered as a teenager.

Harriet had built her life around her symptoms of brain injury. When the sleeping spells came over her, there was nothing she could do to stop them. But when they ended, and she awoke, she jumped back into action. The visions and dreams she experienced might have overwhelmed another person, but Harriet interpreted them as divine guidance, leading her down the path towards freedom for herself and her people. Her headaches were fierce, but she pressed on in spite of them.

As she aged, though, the symptoms grew steadily worse. She came to a point in the 1890s when the seizures were getting worse, the head pain was becoming excruciating, and she could no longer sleep at all. She talked to a doctor at Massachusetts General Hospital in Boston about the problems she was having. She told him of her childhood head injury and that she believed the injury was to blame for her current sleeplessness and pain.

The doctor agreed. He scheduled her for brain surgery. When Harriet was taken into the operating room, she refused anesthesia or pain medications of any kind. Instead, according to the legend, she bit on bullets to distract herself from the pain. When the operation was over, she felt relief from her symptoms and said her head was more comfortable afterward.

As the years passed, Harriet became increasingly frail and prone to illness. She was eventually admitted to the Harriet Tubman Home for Indigent and Aged

Colored People that she had founded years before. There, she was taken care of well and often visited by friends and family members. She continued to express interest in current social problems and often regaled visitors with stories of her life.

On March 10, 1913, Harriet Tubman died in the rest home she helped create. Harriet had lived for more than 90 years. The final illness that took her away was pneumonia.

Before she died, Harriet conducted her own memorial service, singing along with the rest of the people in attendance - when the coughing did not interfere. She sent messages for all the churches to give them her love. Just before she passed on, she told the group of friends and family that had come to share her last moments that "I go to prepare a place for you." At that, she was ready to go; her work finally completed. She laid down and died quietly and peacefully.

Harriet's funeral brought a large number of mourners who came to pay their respects to the woman who had helped them, promoted their cause, or freed their families from slavery. The funeral took place at the Zion A.M.E. Church in Auburn. Semi-military honors were included, at the Fort Hill Cemetery in Auburn when she was buried, to commemorate her service in the Civil War.

The national press, Harriet's abolitionist and suffragist friends, and those who knew her best understood that a great presence had inhabited the earth for a time before moving on. And so, the country mourned the loss of an almost legendary figure in American history.

Chapter 16

Legacy and Tributes

Harriet Tubman's life and achievements provide a legacy of faith in the power of action. She has become a role model for African Americans during their struggle for civil rights and equality under the law. Indeed, she serves as a role model for all who seek to improve social conditions around the world.

At the time of Tubman's death, the city of Auburn made a plaque that included a list of her achievements and message to the world. It was dedicated in a beautiful ceremony to honor her life. Booker T. Washington not only attended but even gave the keynote address.

Frederick Douglass, along with many of her other influential friends, wrote letters to the public, acknowledging her determination to end slavery and the personal skills, talents, and wit she put to work to accomplish her goals. An outpouring of love and appreciation came from around the world to focus on the life of this amazing African American woman.

Historians continue to study the life of Harriet Tubman. Books have been written to describe her. Paintings, wood cuttings, drawings, and other artistic works bear her image and depictions of her deeds. Her character is stamped indelibly on the American consciousness.

All through the 1900s, people and institutions honored the name of Harriet Tubman. Many schools were named in her honor. The house Harriet and Nelson Davis shared was turned into a national museum. The U.S. Maritime Commission named a Liberty ship after her. She was featured on a postage stamp in 1978.

In 1999, a gravestone was set up for her and listed in the National Register of Historic Places. The same year, Canada recognized the Salem Chapel at St. Catharines as a National Historic Site in her honor, and Boston put up a statue of her.

The tributes continued into the 21st century. In 2002, Tubman was included on a scholar's list of the 100 Greatest African Americans. More statues of her were placed, one in Manhattan in 2008, and one at Salisbury University in 2009. President Obama signed a proclamation to establish a national monument to the Underground Railroad, named in her honor in 2013. In 2014, an asteroid was named for her.

By 2028, a new $20 bill will bear her likeness, a fact that has resulted in intense controversy over what picture of her to place on the bill. The bill is being designed at the time of this writing.

There can be no doubt, then, that Harriet Tubman had a profound influence on the world. However, it is not the external tributes that would have mattered most to her. She was a person who valued human rights and human dignity above all else. She would probably have been most pleased with the effect her life made on the lives of African Americans, women, and other oppressed groups.

At times, Harriet Tubman had a fantastic gift for rallying influential people to support her causes. But, at other times, she stood alone against cruelty and injustice. Harriet Tubman may have died more than 100 years ago, but the citizens of the world have certainly not forgotten her. She was indeed an American icon and a world treasure.

Conclusion

One of the most important conclusions to draw from Harriet Tubman's life is a message of hope against all the odds and bravery in the face of whatever obstacles and dangers one encounters. Yet this one powerful woman has taught the world so much more.

Harriet illustrated the benefits of being observant and ready to learn. During her time as a slave, she learned from her mother the value of standing up against the cruelties of slavery. While she was working in the forests and later during her time as a conductor on the Underground Railroad, she used her eyes and ears to find her way, observing the movements of animals and other people to stay safe. As a spy for the Union Army, her powers of observation came into play every day.

One of Harriet Tubman's greatest strengths was her ability to make friends and develop networks of cooperation. This ability served her well on the Railroad and with the Army. Modern people often talk about networking to improve business success. Harriet used her network to gain funding for her causes, but she also had a deeper purpose for her connections. She used them to help other people, and we can still do that today, even though there are no longer any slaves to free.

Another trait of Harriet's that could be tied to business success is her determination to get what she wanted by going to the people who had the power to get things done. We need to remember, though, that what she wanted was for her noble causes to succeed, not just to get more money in her pocket or more fame for the things she did.

Harriet was not stopped by any of her physical limitations. A sickly child, Harriet pushed herself to grow up strong and fit. She was only 5 feet tall, but she took advantage of every inch of her height. When she was injured at 15, she could have reacted to the physical trauma and its after-effects by becoming a virtual invalid. Instead, she followed her heart despite headaches, sleeping spells, and seizures. She could have used these problems as excuses for sitting on the sidelines as others took on the job of helping people in need, but that was not Harriet's way.

Harriet laughed often and sang to her audiences' delight. She lived a great life in a big way. If everyone could accomplish as much for noble causes while keeping their spirits intact, the world would quickly become a more delightful place to live.

Printed in Great Britain
by Amazon